Titanosaur Treasure

by Anne Miranda
illustrated by Ralph Canaday

Harcourt
Orlando Boston Dallas Chicago San Diego

Visit *The Learning Site!*
www.harcourtschool.com

The Thrill of It All

Can you imagine breaking through a stone wall and finding an Egyptian tomb? Imagine finding one filled with wonderful things no one has seen for thousands of years. Can you imagine searching the dark ocean floor? You might find an abandoned sunken ship filled with cargo from an ancient Greek port.

Can you imagine digging up an army of clay statues buried by a Chinese emperor? What a thrill! Many people work their entire lives for such a moment. The possibility of such a valuable find beckons them to continue searching.

On the other hand, do you think someone would be thrilled by finding an egg? Egg hunting doesn't sound exciting, but what if you found a very special egg?

In 1997, a multicultural team of people went on a treasure hunt. Some of them were from the United States, and some were from Argentina. They weren't looking for gold. Instead, they were looking for really, really old bones. These treasure hunters were paleontologists. A paleontologist is a scientist who studies dinosaur bones and other remains of these ancient creatures.

The team went to a new land for a special reason. They traveled to Patagonia to hunt for treasure. Patagonia is in the southern part of Argentina, where few people live. Often such spots are good places to find fossils because people have not disturbed the land. Also, fossils survive best in a dry climate. Water can wash away or damage fossils. Patagonia is dry, a perfect spot for their treasure hunt.

Getting Started

The team of fourteen paleontologists had planned their trip for a long time. They had gathered food and equipment and paid their air fares. They set off in November 1997. It was fall in the Northern Hemisphere but spring in Patagonia. The team met in Buenos Aires, Argentina, and drove to the dig site.

A dig site is a place where scientists dig for "treasure." Sometimes they dig to learn more about an ancient town that used to exist on that spot. In this case, the treasure was dinosaur bones.

The year before, these scientists had found fossils of sauropods in another dig site. It was near where they were heading. Sauropods are huge, plant-eating dinosaurs.

It was a 14-hour drive from Buenos Aires to the rugged land of Patagonia. The dig site was near an extinct volcano. The site had no hotels or houses. There were no kitchens, bathrooms, or running water. There weren't even any beds! This was, indeed, a place where few people lived.

The scientists had to cook outdoors and sleep on the hard ground. They lived in tents, one for each person. Creepy, crawly things, such as tarantulas, seemed to think the tents made cozy shelters. The scientists had to watch out for overnight guests. Who wants to have a pajama party with a big hairy spider?

Days 1 and 2

After they set up camp, the scientists quickly began to look for fossils. They inspected the ground, hoping to find part of a bone or a tooth. They also looked for dinosaur footprints that had hardened into rock. They hoped to find evidence that dinosaurs had lived in the area.

This way of fossil hunting is called prospecting. To be a good prospector, a scientist has to know what to look for. It takes years of training to tell a bone from a stick or a tooth from a rock.

On the first day, the scientists found nothing. However, they were used to that. Dinosaur fossils don't just lie all over the ground, do they?

Day 2 was much more profitable. It was a day that paleontologists dream of but rarely experience. They began to prospect a few miles from their camp. Suddenly, a team member spotted something lying on the ground. It was gray like a stone and round like a shell. However, it had bumps all over its surface, unlike any stone the scientists had seen. Could it possibly be a dinosaur egg? Yes, it was! The scientists were thrilled!

They actually found hundreds of grapefruit-size dinosaur eggs that had turned to stone. To the paleontologists, finding the eggs was like finding gold. So many eggs covered the ground that it was hard not to step on them.

The Mysteries

The scientists were certain they had found dinosaur eggs. However, they had two mysteries to solve. Why were so many eggs in one place? What kind of dinosaurs had laid them?

The first mystery was fairly easy to solve. The scientists already knew that some dinosaurs laid eggs in nests that were very close together. These dinosaurs nested in colonies. Gathering in big groups to lay eggs and protect their babies helped the dinosaurs survive. By staying together, the adults could help defend each other. They could also take turns guarding the young. This freed other adults to leave and look for food.

The scientists knew they had found the nesting site of thousands of dinosaurs. It covered acres of land. Why had the eggs not hatched?

The scientists thought that something terrible must have happened—and suddenly. Perhaps it began with a long, heavy rain. The river nearby might have flooded over its banks. The flood could have buried the eggs in mud. Then the babies inside the eggs died.

The eggs stayed under the mud for millions of years. During this time, the wind gradually blew away the dry mud and uncovered the eggs. The scientists wondered if a skeleton of a baby dinosaur had been preserved in an egg. If so, they could solve the second big mystery: what kind of dinosaurs had laid the eggs?

The Miracles

Until this fossil hunt, only five dinosaur embryos (unborn baby dinosaurs) had ever been found. Why so few? Dinosaur embryos are very small and delicate.

For example, the apatosaurus was a 70-foot-long sauropod that weighed tons. However, the females laid eggs only the size of grapefruits. The baby may have been only a foot long when it hatched. Baby dinosaur bones and teeth are small and delicate. Finding them preserved is almost impossible.

Yet sometimes almost-impossible things do happen. The scientists found a skeleton inside one of the eggs! They hoped to study the bones and find out what kind of dinosaur had laid the egg.

In time, the scientists found other eggs with bones inside them. They even found eggs that contained the skin of a baby dinosaur. No scientist had ever found preserved soft tissue of a dinosaur. (Soft tissues are muscles, organs, and skin.) Usually only the hard bones and teeth are preserved.

The news of their find quickly traveled to scientists and others around the world. At last, we would know what a dinosaur really looked like. Everyone had wondered if dinosaur skin was smooth or scaly.

The skin found inside the egg was scaly, like a lizard's. A kind of stripe ran along the baby's back. One more dinosaur mystery had been solved. Now the scientists wondered how the skin had been preserved.

How Fossils Form

When a dinosaur died, its soft tissue rotted away or was eaten by animals. However, hard bones and teeth take a long time to decay. If the skeleton became covered by dust or mud, the bones might fossilize.

Fossilization takes a long time. Minerals in the soil replace the decayed parts of the bones, turning the bones into stone. Fossilized bones consist of mineral replacements of the actual bone.

Fossils are often embedded in rock or buried deep in the Earth. When Earth's crust moves, fossils may be brought closer to the surface. If the rock around the fossils wears away, the fossils become exposed and are sometimes found by people.

When the dinosaur eggs were buried in the flood, it probably happened very quickly. The mud must have been thick and deep. It was too deep for the parents to dig up and rescue their eggs.

The thick mud did not allow oxygen to get to the eggs. This lack of oxygen slowed down the decay process. Then mud oozed through cracks in the dinosaur eggs. Minerals in the mud slowly turned the tiny bones and teeth to stone.

Amazingly, the mud also preserved some embryo skin. The mud that killed the baby dinosaurs also preserved their tiny embryos for millions of years.

What Were They?

The scientists still could not tell what kind of dinosaur had laid the eggs. They were fairly sure they were sauropod eggs. To be certain, the eggs would be shipped to the United States and examined more closely.

Each egg was carefully dug up and wrapped in plaster bandages. Most of the eggs were sent to the museum where the scientists worked. Some were sent to a university. There, scientists would open them and compare the bones with fossils of known dinosaurs.

A few weeks after they had arrived in Patagonia, the paleontologists were ready to go home. They were excited to find out what kind of dinosaur had laid the eggs they found.

However, the scientists had to wait a few months for the answer to this mystery. First, a scientist called a preparator spent weeks chipping away the rock around each tiny bone in each tiny egg. This work is done with a needle under a microscope. You can imagine how long this might take. The preparator works slowly to avoid damaging the fragile bones.

After a month or so, the preparator discovered the key that unlocked the mystery. She found a tiny skull and some teeny tiny teeth. She compared the small bones, skull, and teeth to those of adult dinosaurs. The mystery was solved: the dinosaur's parents were titanosaurs.

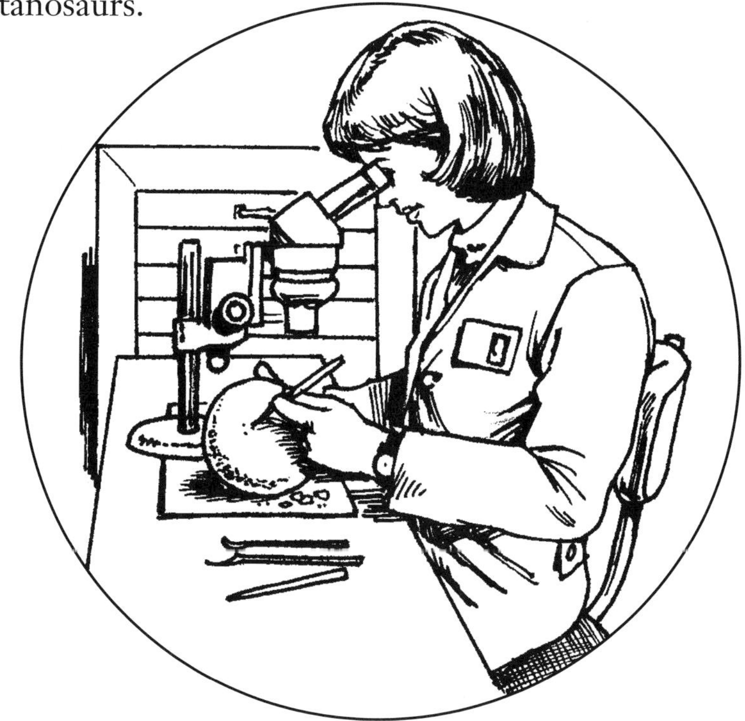

Titanosaurs

The titanosaur was a huge plant-eating dinosaur. It had a heavy body, a long tail, a long neck, and a small head. At about 50 feet long, it must have looked like a truck!

The newly hatched titanosaurs would have seemed like toys next to their huge parents. Imagine a dinosaur small enough to carry in a backpack!

Titanosaurs laid eggs in nests and cared for their babies much like birds do today. Scientists think titanosaurs brought food back to the nests. They may have fed their babies food they had already digested. Birds and other animals feed their babies this way.

The paleontologists had traveled a long way to a new land. They discovered a treasure that no one had seen before. Who knows what they might discover next?